It's the Little Things

300 Simple
Ways to Indulge
Yourself

AMY COLLINS

Published by
Adams Media Corporation
57 Littlefield Street, Avon, MA 02322 U.S.A.
www.adamsmedia.com

ISBN: 1-58062-749-8

Printed in Canada.

J I H G F E D C B A

Library of Congress Cataloging-in-Publication Data
Collins, Amy.
It's the little things / by Amy Collins.
p.   cm.
ISBN 1-58062-749-8
1. Happiness. 2. Conduct of life. I. Title.
BF575.H27 C65 2002
158.1—dc21
200200860

This publication is designed to provide accurate and authoritative information with regard to the subject matter covered. It is sold with the understanding that the publisher is not engaged in rendering legal, accounting, or other professional advice. If legal advice or other expert assistance is required, the services of a competent professional person should be sought.
—From a *Declaration of Principles* jointly adopted by a Committee of the American Bar Association and a Committee of Publishers and Associations

Illustrations by Rosanne Raneri.

This book is available at quantity discounts for bulk purchases.
For information, call 1-800-872-5627.

For Rosemary Donoghue,
Beatrice Langdon,
and Faith Donoghue.

Thanks and appreciation to: Rosanne Raneri and Kristi Heitzman, two women who are beautiful examples of how to treat ourselves and others. Thanks to Maura Versluys, Mary Frances Collins, Beth Peters Collins, and the rest of my amazing family for their ideas and encouragement. I am very grateful to Bethany Brown, Tara TenEyck, Kerry Farrell, Carrie Lewis-McGraw, Kate McBride, Rachael Eiben, Jennifer Wolfe, and Susan Beale. All of these women shared their secret and not-so-secret indulgences with me and inspire me daily. Finally, thank you to Claire Gerus, Scott Watrous, Bob Adams, Gary Krebs, and everyone at Adams Media Corporation.

"Don't know who I'm racing with,
but pretty sure I'm losing.
Don't know where I'm going,
but pretty sure I'm late."

Sound familiar? All the rushing around, all the catching up, and all the listing off we do can leave us feeling unconnected and drained. We all feel the need to re-energize, reconnect, and relax—but how?

It's the Little Things offers 300 simple, easy ways to help us reclaim a very precious gift: the ability to enjoy the "small indulgences" that will bring beauty, peace, and sensuality back into our frenzied days.

May every day offer you the opportunity to enjoy at least one "little thing" that lifts your heart.

Amy Collins

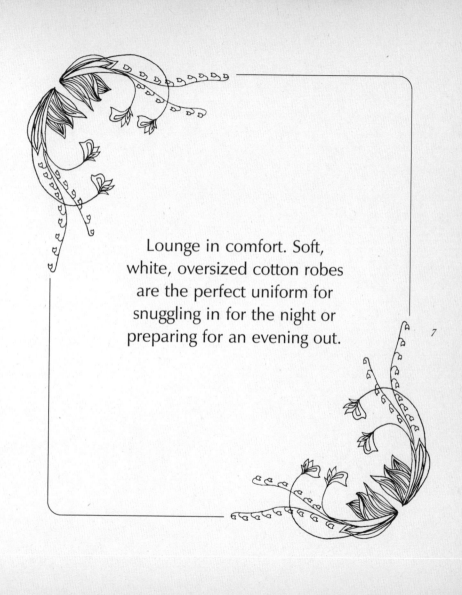

Lounge in comfort. Soft,
white, oversized cotton robes
are the perfect uniform for
snuggling in for the night or
preparing for an evening out.

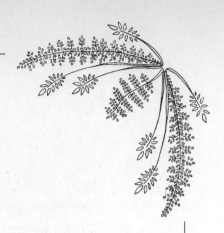

When it comes to coffee,
ice cream, and cookies,
go for the best.

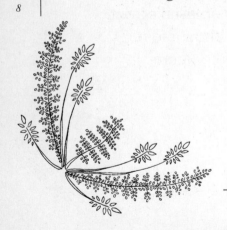

Turn off the lights and spend
an evening in candlelight.
The flickering shadows create
a softened world that shifts
your focus and helps you relax.
Feel yourself wind down as
you enjoy the blissful silence
of a world without radio, TV,
or your computer.

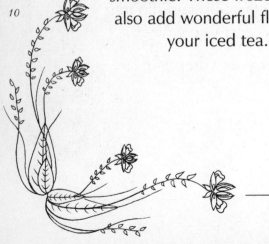

Pour your favorite juice into ice cube trays and freeze. Drop a few cubes into the blender every time you want a refreshing smoothie. These frozen treats also add wonderful flavor to your iced tea.

Massage your hands with a fragrant hand cream right before you go to sleep. You will soon associate this ritual and fragrance with relaxation and slip into sleep more easily.

11

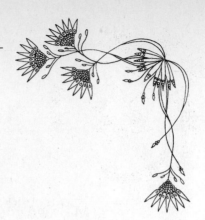

Make brownies a regular part of
your mental health routine.

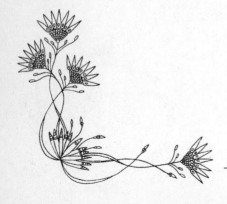

Go to bed an hour early
and get up fifteen minutes
earlier in the morning.
Your body will appreciate the
extra sleep and your mind
needs the few extra minutes
in the morning.

"*Indulge:*
To take unrestrained
pleasure in."

—*Merriam–Webster*
Collegiate Dictionary

Take out that favorite piece of
jewelry that you usually save for
"special occasions." Every day is
a special occasion, isn't it?

15

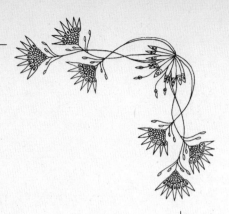

Improve your "car"-ma. Let
another driver into traffic in front
of you. And be sure to smile and
wave if someone lets you in.

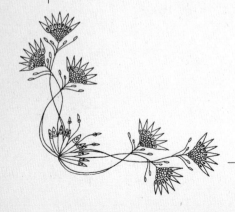

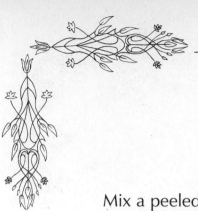

Mix a peeled, pitted plum with your favorite heavy face cream in the blender. Apply this fruited mask to your face and neck for ten minutes. It evens out your complexion while giving your skin a nutritious boost.

Say "no" when you want to.

Say "yes" when you want to.

Always keep a disposable camera close by—be ready to capture a special moment.

Trade in your bath towels for thick, colorful bath sheets and stack them in a basket beside the tub.

19

"The only way to get rid of a
temptation is to yield to it."

—Oscar Wilde (1854–1900)

Hang out at your local bookstore. Grab a cup of decaf and settle in a comfy chair, or browse through the shelves of your favorite section.

Create your own favorite coffee mug at a design-your-own pottery studio.

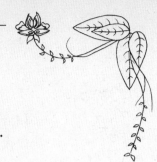

Savor a sunset.

For a quick fresh-baked treat,
keep a roll of cookie dough
in the freezer. Slice off a
section and use the microwave
or toaster oven to bake a
fresh, hot cookie or two.

"Joy:
A vivid emotion of
pleasure arising from
a sense of well-being."

—*Oxford-American Dictionary*

23

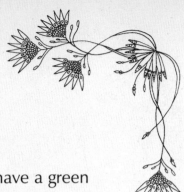

Everyone can have a green thumb. Plant shamrock seeds and put four ice cubes on top of the soil to allow for slow watering. Four more ice cubes every other day will bear great results. You, too, may develop the luck of the Irish!

Don't answer the telephone
when you don't want to talk.

Do you have a teddy bear? Soft,
loyal, cuddly, discreet . . . the
perfect companion when you
need some TLC.

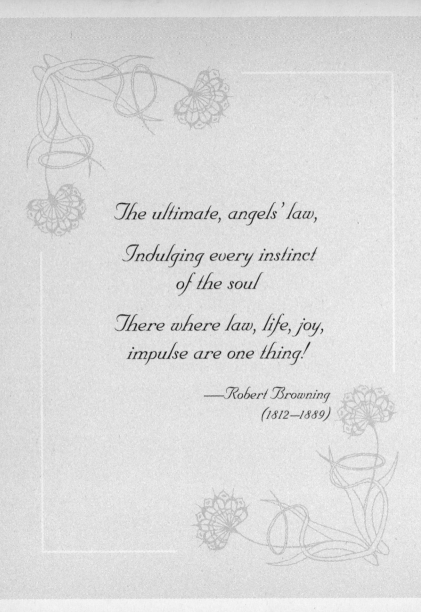

The ultimate, angels' law,

*Indulging every instinct
of the soul*

*There where law, life, joy,
impulse are one thing!*

——*Robert Browning*
(1812—1889)

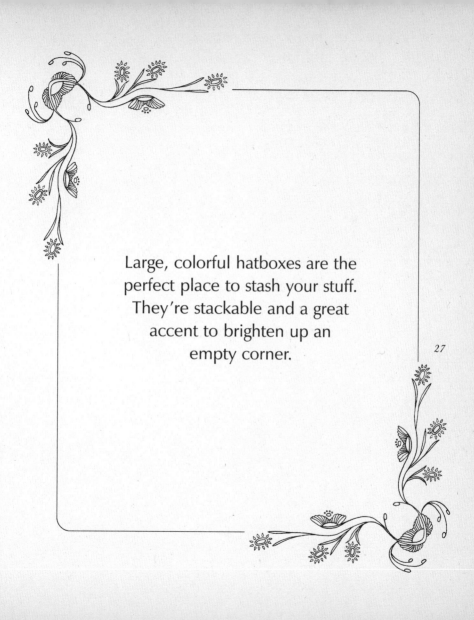

Large, colorful hatboxes are the perfect place to stash your stuff. They're stackable and a great accent to brighten up an empty corner.

Find a piece of art that you
love and place it where you
can enjoy it the most.

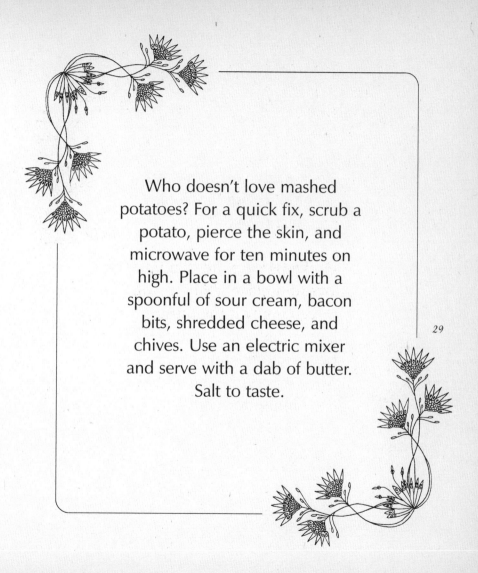

Who doesn't love mashed potatoes? For a quick fix, scrub a potato, pierce the skin, and microwave for ten minutes on high. Place in a bowl with a spoonful of sour cream, bacon bits, shredded cheese, and chives. Use an electric mixer and serve with a dab of butter. Salt to taste.

29

Pick a city you've always
wanted to visit, and enjoy
planning the trip.

Fill your bath with fresh flower
petals and floating candles.
They'll perfume the whole
house for hours.

"*How wrong it is for a woman
to expect the man to build the
world she wants, rather than
to create it herself.*"

—*Anaïs Nin (1903–1977)*

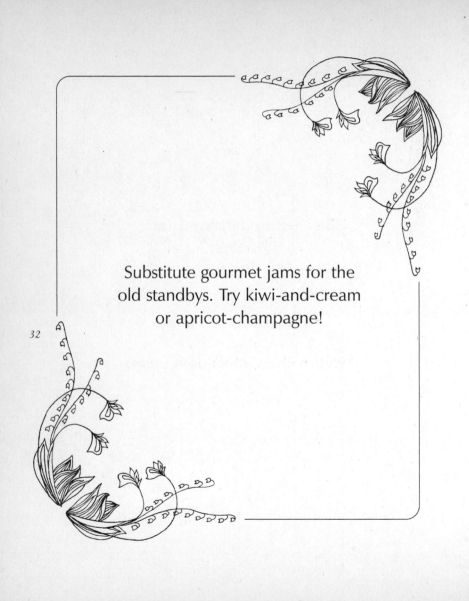

Substitute gourmet jams for the
old standbys. Try kiwi-and-cream
or apricot-champagne!

Tuck yourself into a warm,
soft, down comforter.

Sleep with your window open.

Listen to your body.

Are you hungry? Eat.

Are you thirsty? Drink.

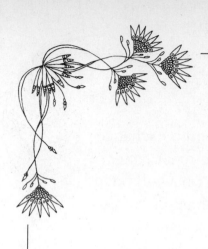

Are you tired? Rest.

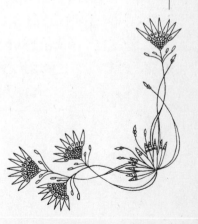

Isn't it more fun to exchange letters than e-mail? Letter writing doesn't have to be a chore. Buy a sheet of stamps; creamy, thick stationery; gorgeous postcards; a stack of birthday cards; and a heavy pen. Place them in a beautiful old box on your desk or table. Write one friend a week. Postcards are perfect when you are busy, letters for when you have more time.

Get a professional pedicure.
Treat your feet.

Kids napping? Join them!

Choose the scenic
way home.

Clean out your closet. Get rid
of anything that doesn't
make you feel fabulous!

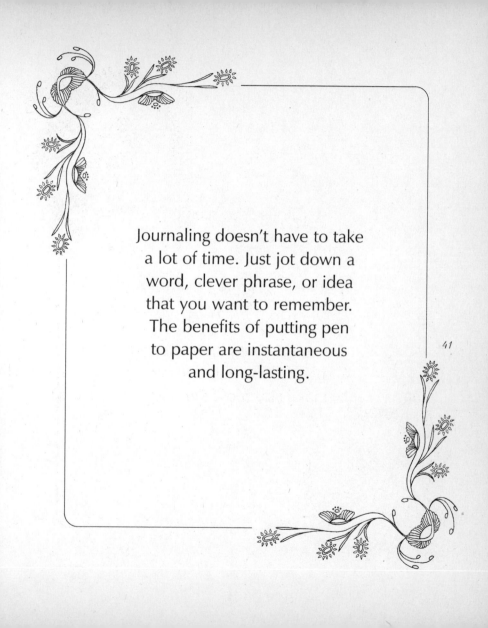

Journaling doesn't have to take a lot of time. Just jot down a word, clever phrase, or idea that you want to remember. The benefits of putting pen to paper are instantaneous and long-lasting.

"*Treat:*
To give (someone or oneself)
something pleasurable."

—*Oxford–American Dictionary*

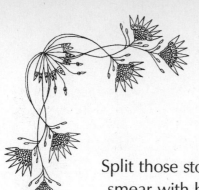

Split those store-bought muffins, smear with butter, and toast in the oven until crispy brown.

Indulge your whimsical side. Slide across the kitchen floor in your socks.

Feeling stressed? Relax with a "Zen breathing square." Inhale slowly to the count of four. Hold it for four beats. Exhale as you count to four again. Finally, hold the exhale for four beats. Repeat until you feel your shoulders drop and your back relax.

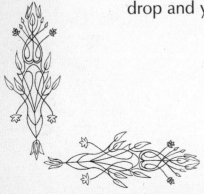

Go to the five-and-dime and
buy some bubbles. Then, get out
that wand and start blowing!

45

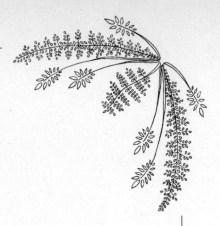

Own at least one silk
or satin nightie.

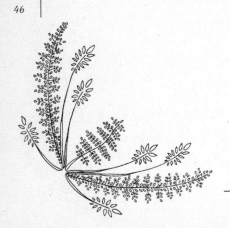

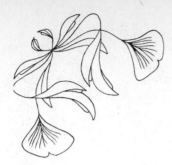

Own at least two pairs
of flannel PJs.

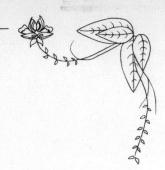

To smooth knees and elbows,
cut a lemon in half and massage
it over the rough spots. Finish
with a thick moisturizing cream.

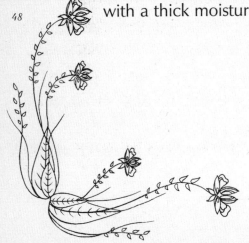

Relax with your favorite drink
on your front porch or stoop.

Read your horoscope
every day.

Find the thickest, softest throw
rug you can and make sure it's
the first thing your
feet feel in the morning.
Get another one for the bath.

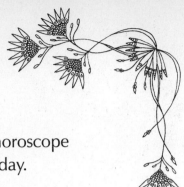

Visit your local drugstore and try
out a new kind of makeup.

Get yourself a nice, big, comfy chair with a table for your book and drink. Put a floor lamp behind the chair, and face it toward a window or your favorite work of art.

Remember how good real popcorn can be? Use a light oil and go easy on the salt . . . it tastes great and is better for you than the chemical, microwave kind.

53

Don't bring work home
from the office.

Stop at a full-serve gas
station and treat yourself
to a little extra service.

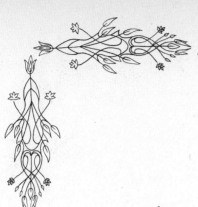

Laugh every day. Choose a
comic strip that makes you grin.
Keep one near you at home,
and another pinned up at
the office so it'll be there
when you need it.

Enjoy the weather. Go play
in the snow, walk in the rain,
bask in the sun . . .

Pull it together. A large wicker basket on your countertop is the perfect place to store all of your beauty products. The neat, clean look soothes your senses as you get ready for your day.

Treat Sunday as the one day a
week when you don't have to
be somewhere or do something.
Stay home and relax.

Enhance any beauty experience.
Put up a shelf just for candles in
your bathroom. Put up another
in your bedroom!

Stop and ignore the roses.
Buy an exotic, dramatic,
hard-to-pronounce flower
and a funky vase for your
desk or kitchen table.

59

"*Fill what's empty, empty what's full,
and scratch where it itches.*"

——*The Duchess of Windsor,
when asked for the secret of
a long and happy life*

Choose your favorite color and
paint just one wall. It makes
such a difference, it only takes a
bit of time, and you won't have
to move all your furniture.

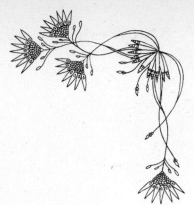

Buy a fish and keep it on your desk at work to remind you of what is really important. Water, movement, and breathing are all you truly need.

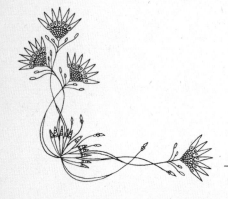

Enjoy the perfect cinnamon toast: three parts sugar to one part cinnamon. Mix and sprinkle on lightly buttered, toasted bread.

Go live! Stop by your local club
for some live music, pop into
a gallery to see the exhibit, or
pick up tickets for a play.

Keep a "dream book" by your
bed so you can jot down your
dreams from the night before.

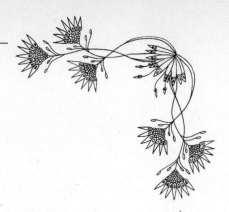

Find a favorite pen and always
keep it on you. Even writing
checks can be a treat!

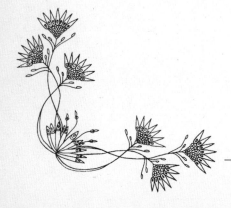

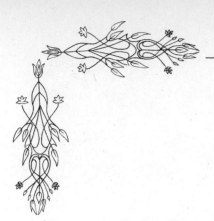

Soft, silk scarves feel fabulous and drift gorgeously over your shoulders. Spritz one with your favorite scent and add a little pizzazz to your day.

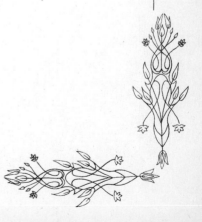

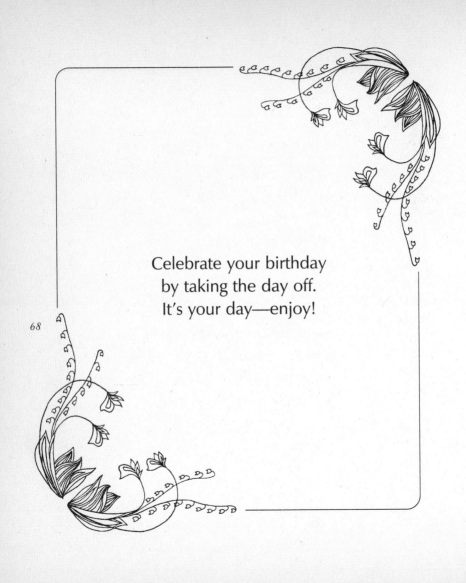

Celebrate your birthday
by taking the day off.
It's your day—enjoy!

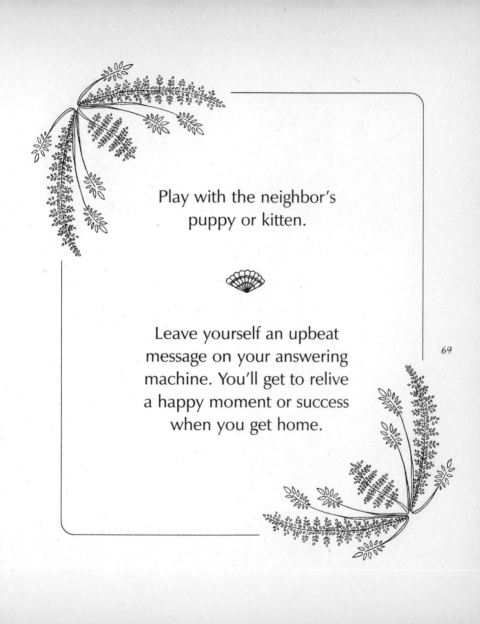

Play with the neighbor's
puppy or kitten.

Leave yourself an upbeat
message on your answering
machine. You'll get to relive
a happy moment or success
when you get home.

69

Reread your old love letters.

There's more than one way to save for a rainy day. Purchase a gift certificate for yourself at your favorite store, then tuck it away for those tight months when you need a little pick-me-up.

71

Plan a board game evening
with family or friends. Share
the laughter and a little
healthy competition.

*"Nothing can bring you
peace but yourself."*

——*Ralph Waldo Emerson
(1803–1882)*

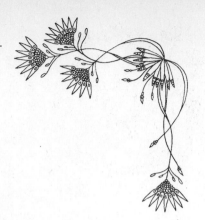

Post an affirmation or
happy thought on your mirror.
Start your day off in the
right frame of mind.

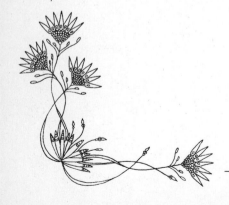

Dig out those old boxes of
photos and revel in your past.

Spray your favorite perfume
on a few cotton balls and tuck
into your dresser drawers.
A fresh bloom of scent greets
you with each opening.

Say "hello" to the person
behind you in line.

Don't want the fuss and mess of a fire in your fireplace? Arrange twelve to fifteen pillar candles of varying heights to flicker and soothe. Evergreen candles are perfect for Christmas, bayberry for spring, and cinnamon for fall.

Create your own celebration.
Dress up in your favorite outfit
and meet your favorite friends
downtown for a drink.

Create a cocoon. Spend an
entire day in your room.
Take your meals, phone
calls, and books to bed.

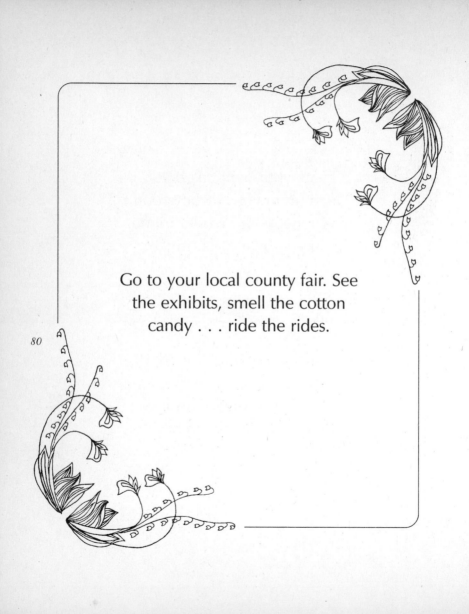

Go to your local county fair. See
the exhibits, smell the cotton
candy . . . ride the rides.

On a cold winter night, throw your sheets in the dryer for a few minutes, make up your bed quickly, and then crawl into the toasty goodness.

Find a favorite photo, blow
it up, and place it in an
attractive frame.

Mix and match fragrances—a
little spice, a little floral—until
you've created the perfect
scent, just for you.

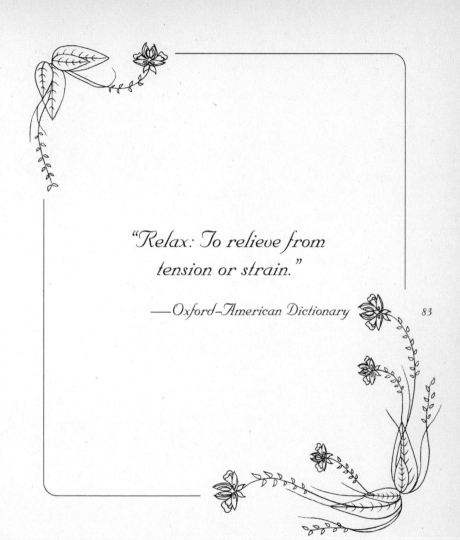

"Relax: To relieve from tension or strain."

—*Oxford–American Dictionary*

Maybe you can't afford a weekly cleaning service, but you *can* get your house cleaned by a professional crew once in a while. Let them get the corners and the hard-to-reach places. Come home to a clean, wonderfully smelling house.

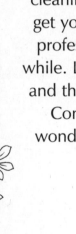

84

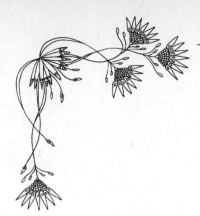

Write a letter or call an old
childhood friend, no matter how
long it's been. Reconnect with
your past if only for a moment.

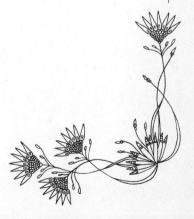

Pamper your car. Get it
cleaned inside and out.
Splurge on the mat shampoos
and crevice cleaning for
that "new car" feeling.

"There is no sincerer love
than the love of food."

—George Bernard Shaw
(1856–1950)

Bury the hatchet today. Write a letter forgiving one person. You don't have to mail it; just writing it down will free your spirit.

Try yoga. Anyone can benefit from the gentle stretching and limbering exercises. It takes so little to feel so good!

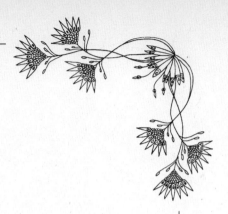

Replace your morning coffee
with a healthy mug of green tea.

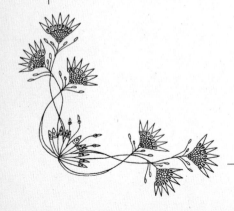

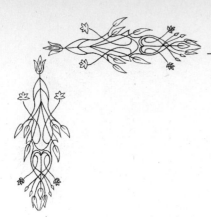

New sheets and pillowcases
can make bedtime a blissful
experience. Buy a set of
400-count Egyptian cotton
sheets for a sense of real luxury.

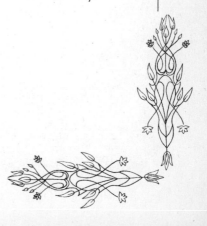

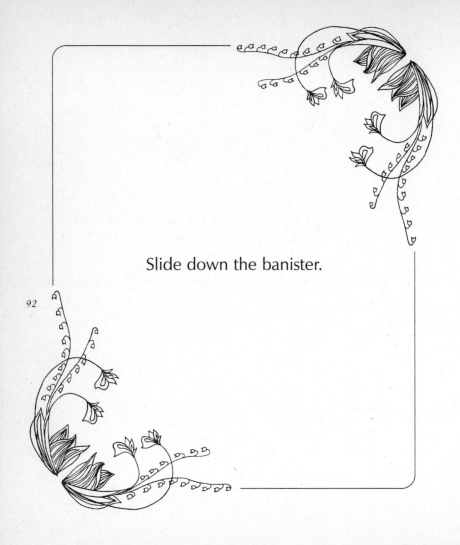

Slide down the banister.

"True enjoyment comes from
activity of the mind and
exercise of the body;
the two are ever united."

—Wilhelm von Humboldt
(1767–1835)

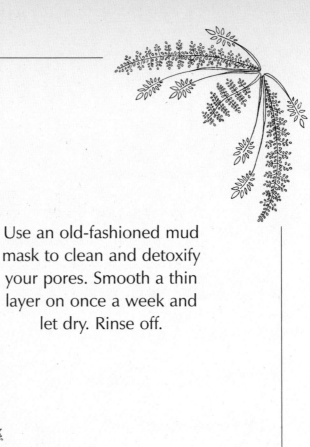

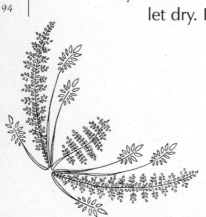

Use an old-fashioned mud mask to clean and detoxify your pores. Smooth a thin layer on once a week and let dry. Rinse off.

For a perfect picnic, pack oranges, stoned cracked-wheat crackers, iced shrimp, and a little cheese. Bring a blanket, eat, lie back, look around, breathe, listen.

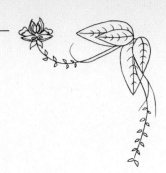

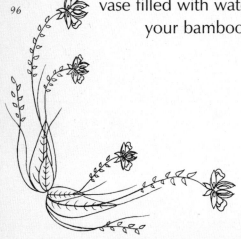

Tall spiraling stalks of bamboo
rising from a clear glass vase
bring beauty and energy into
your home or office. Keep the
vase filled with water and watch
your bamboo grow!

Sleep naked.

The recipe for a perfect day:
Find a canoe or rowboat, plan
to soak in the sun for three
hours, add water, and stir.

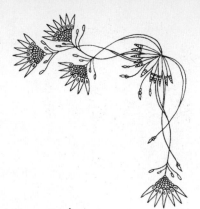

To your health! Mix cranberry
or orange juice with club
soda or seltzer. Unlike soda,
it ups your vitamins and
lowers your caffeine intake.

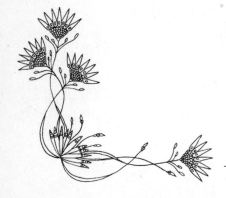

Try a new recipe and serve it
on your favorite dinnerware—
just for you.

Shine up your jewelry! Stop by a professional jeweler, or buy an inexpensive cleaning solution. In just a few minutes, your jewelry will look like new.

Plan a weekly "gab-fest" with your best friend. No matter how busy you are, spending time together is more important.

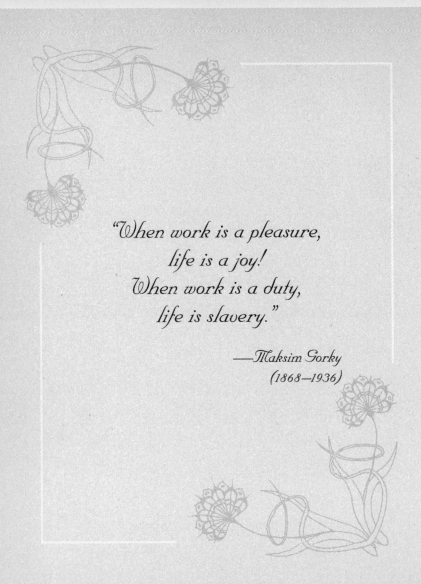

"When work is a pleasure,
life is a joy!
When work is a duty,
life is slavery."

——Maksim Gorky
(1868–1936)

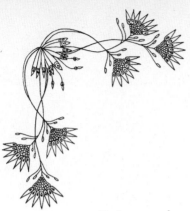

Enjoy a cleansing and refreshing
shower experience using a
brass rain-shower fixture
that gives you that waterfall
feeling at home.

Listen to a tape of your favorite
comedian on your way to work.

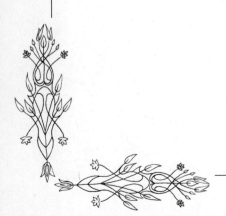

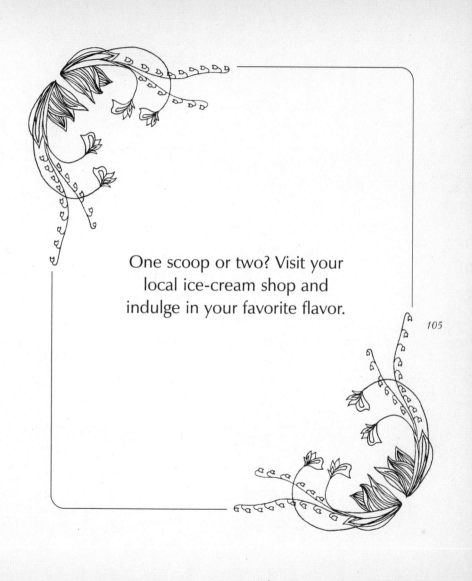

One scoop or two? Visit your local ice-cream shop and indulge in your favorite flavor.

For the ultimate in relaxation,
walk the beach and pick
up some seashells. Then,
pick out your favorite and
leave the rest behind for
another beach-walker.

Have breakfast in bed with your
favorite magazine or newspaper.

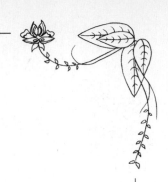

Carry a vial or two of fragrant oils, such as lavender or vanilla musk, to dab on during the day. They're instant mood-enhancers!

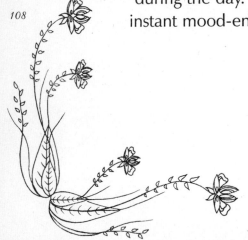

Sing! In the car, in the shower, in the kitchen, in the supermarket . . . join in with the music on the radio or in your head. It's a great way to loosen up the spirit.

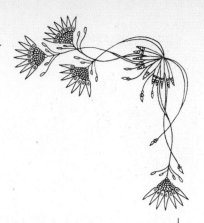

Instead of walking around a
sprinkler, just dash right through.

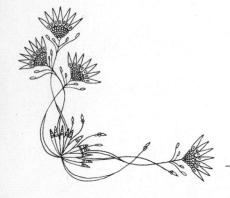

Beautiful glassware can
make any drink a celebration.
Pour water or juice into
an elegant wine glass.
It actually tastes better!

Spend an evening in black
and white—movies, that is.
*The Philadelphia Story, Topper,
The African Queen,* or *The Ghost
and Mrs. Muir* are all fine choices.
Slip into another time
period for a few hours.

For an elegant, low-cal dessert, melt your favorite chocolate over low heat, and then dip in your favorite berries. Allow them to cool on wax paper, and then gently tumble them into a champagne flute.

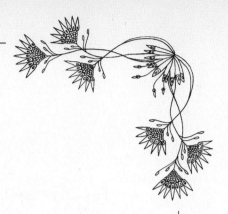

Be a passenger. Let someone
else drive for a change.

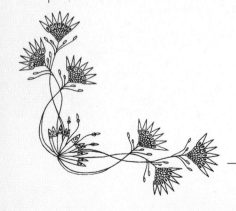

There is a pleasure in the pathless woods;
There is a rapture on the lonely shore;
There is society, where none intrudes,
By the deep sea, and music in its roar:
I love not man the less, but Nature more.

—Lord Byron (1788–1824)

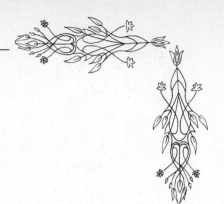

Go out to the country for some peace. Get away from the lights and noise, and discover more stars than you knew existed.

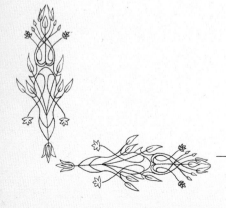

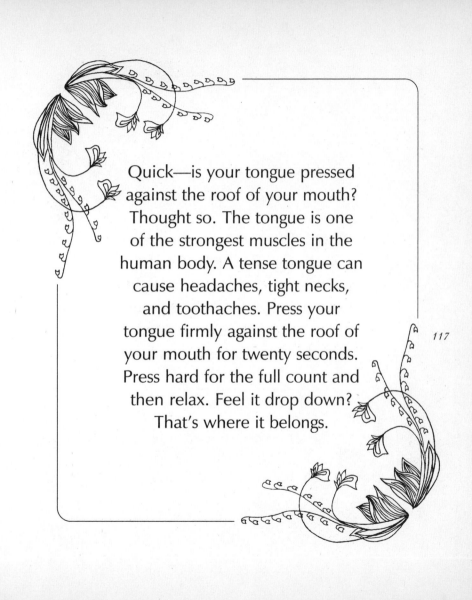

Quick—is your tongue pressed against the roof of your mouth? Thought so. The tongue is one of the strongest muscles in the human body. A tense tongue can cause headaches, tight necks, and toothaches. Press your tongue firmly against the roof of your mouth for twenty seconds. Press hard for the full count and then relax. Feel it drop down? That's where it belongs.

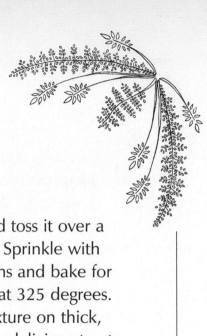

Slice a pear and toss it over a
wedge of brie. Sprinkle with
walnuts or pecans and bake for
twenty minutes at 325 degrees.
Spread the mixture on thick,
crusty bread for a delicious treat.

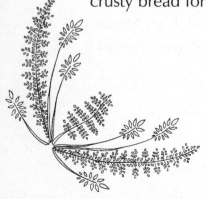

Kick up the autumn leaves.

Have fun learning more about
yourself. The Web sites
www.Ivillage.com and
www.emode.com have fun,
quirky quizzes that you'll enjoy.

Sit by at least one bonfire a year,
preferably on the beach.
Marshmallows, anyone?

Recess! Take a break each
day and make sure to do
something you really enjoy.
Read, sketch, or play a game.

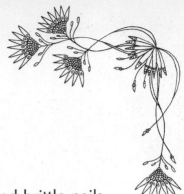

Heal dry hands and brittle nails.
Wisk a fresh egg yolk with
avocado and gently massage
it into your hands. Leave on
for fifteen minutes and rinse
off with warm water.

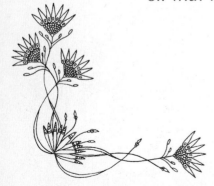

Take a day off from work to do nothing. It's okay to do nothing . . . promise.

123

Check your local bakery for
fruity, nutty, spicy bread.

Take fifteen minutes when you arrive home just for yourself. Leave the groceries on the counter; leave the mail on the table. Change out of your work clothes. Leave the office behind and greet your evening feeling renewed.

125

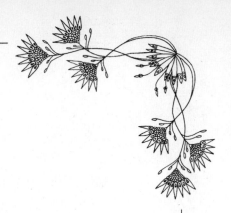

Take one thing off your to-do list this week. Do the same favor for your kids.

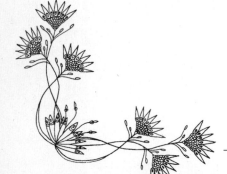

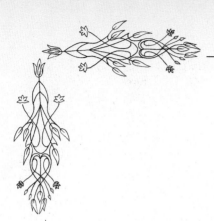

Walk. Walk to get the mail. Walk across the street. Don't waste time looking for a closer parking space. Strut your stuff.

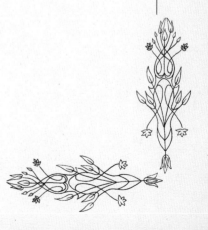

"There are only two ways to live your life: one as if nothing is a miracle, the other as if everything is a miracle."

——*Albert Einstein*
(1879—1955)

Dig through the bargain bin at
your favorite music store.

Visit an Irish pub on St. Patrick's
Day and sing along with the
crowd. "Danny Boy" never
sounded better.

Sneak away from your
daily grind and take in
a weekday matinee.

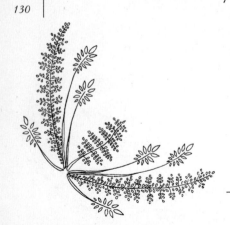

Perk up your favorite handbag.
Local shoe shops can condition,
restitch, and even recolor
your purses to give them
a whole new life.

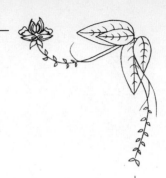

Place vases of fresh flowers in
your bath, bedroom, front hall,
and even your laundry room.

"*A house is a home when it shelters the body and comforts the soul.*"

—Phillip Moffitt

Root beer–barrel candy,
Blow-Pops®, licorice, fireballs,
watermelon gum, and Pixy
Stix® are instant passports to
your childhood. Enjoy.

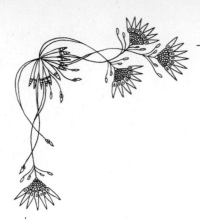

Visit an upscale salon and
splurge on a hair color
consultation. Let an expert show
you how to jazz up the real you.

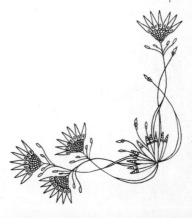

Change the scene for a night
and check into a hotel,
preferably one with a pool.
Swim, read, and sleep. No
phone calls, no beds to make,
and you can have meals
brought right to your room.

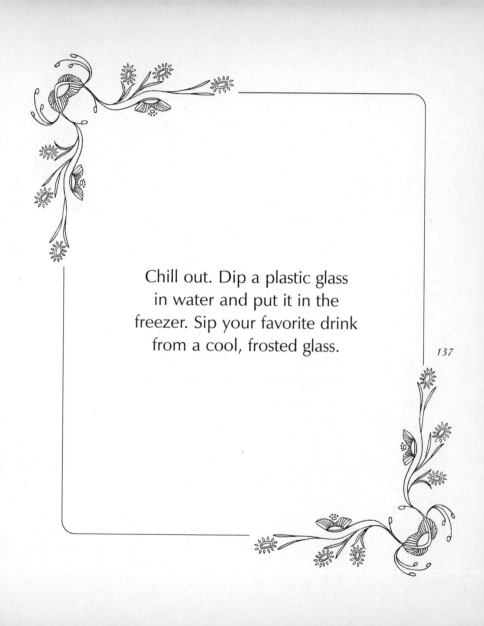

Chill out. Dip a plastic glass
in water and put it in the
freezer. Sip your favorite drink
from a cool, frosted glass.

137

Spend a few minutes each day
looking out the window.

Create your own bathroom spa.
Bring in soft light, music, bath
pillows, and sea salts.

Brighten your smile. There are several affordable, at-home tooth whiteners available today. It's not just hype; whiter teeth do make a difference. You'll smile more!

139

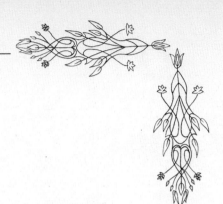

Plant lavender, rosemary, and
sage in pretty glazed clay pots
and place in your eastern and
southern windows. The heat
from the sun releases a heady
burst of aroma each day.

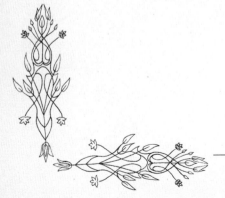

"If you had one hour to live and could only make one call, who would it be to, what would you say, and why are you waiting?"

——*Stephen Levine*

Fluff and fold. Do you really
have to do the laundry? Drop
your week's worth off at a local
full-service laundromat. When
you pick it up the next day, your
shirts will be ironed and the rest
of your clothes will be folded
and ready for the dresser.

Time to do chores? Put on a
Latin music CD or '80s radio
station, turn up the volume,
and feel the beat while you
go through the motions.

Eat at the table.

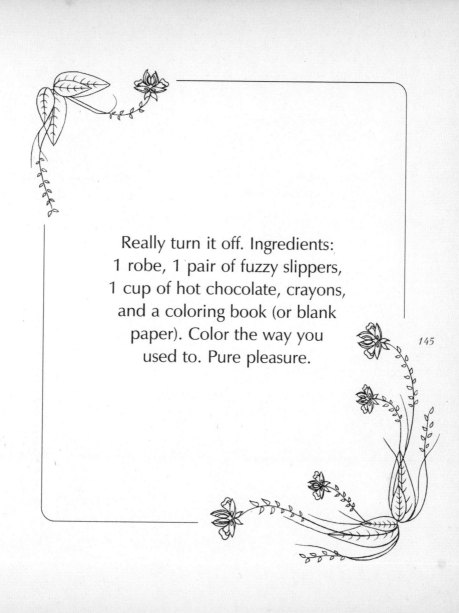

Really turn it off. Ingredients:
1 robe, 1 pair of fuzzy slippers,
1 cup of hot chocolate, crayons,
and a coloring book (or blank
paper). Color the way you
used to. Pure pleasure.

Regress a little. Make a meal
of your favorite childhood
foods. Why not call your
mother for ideas?

Sleep in at least one
morning a week.

Visit a vineyard or brewery.
Take a tour and savor the
local specialties.

"You were made for enjoyment, and the world was filled with things which you will enjoy, unless you are too proud to be pleased with them, or too grasping to care for what you cannot turn to other account than mere delight."

—John Ruskin
(1819–1900)

Enjoy a round of miniature golf.

Get a temporary tattoo.

Bake a cake for no reason!
Place it in a glass-covered
pedestal dish and enjoy the
sight and taste.

Celebrate May Day by picking wildflowers. Tuck one in your hair or behind your ear.

Create your own tropical breezes. Open a bottle of Coppertone® to perfume the room with thoughts of summer.

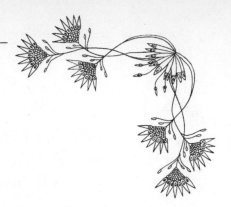

Leave a $20 in the pocket of
your winter coat each spring.
You'll have a wonderful "extra"
when you have to put it on for
the first time next winter.

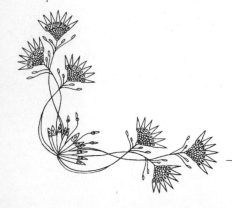

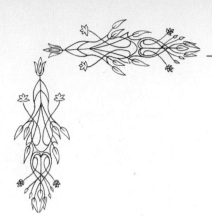

Bring beauty to work. Your favorite works of art can be found on postcards. Set a few of your favorites on your computer or desk.

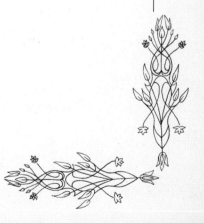

"So of cheerfulness, or a
good temper, the more it is
spent, the more it remains."

——*Ralph Waldo Emerson*
(1803–1882)

Use cloth napkins
and placemats for an
elegant touch at breakfast.

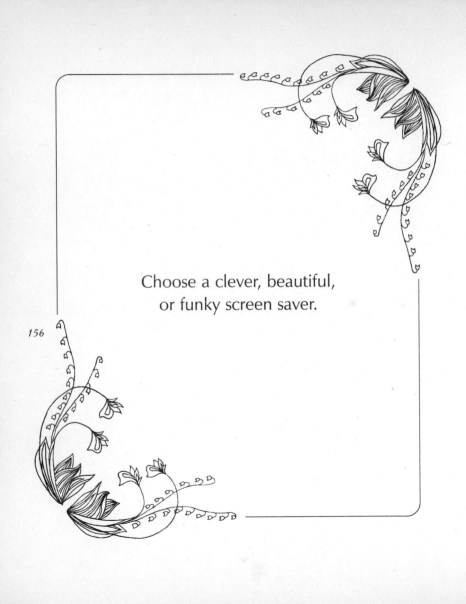

Choose a clever, beautiful,
or funky screen saver.

Wear your favorite
perfume every day.

Share a joke.

Get a Slinky®. It gives your hands
something to do while you wait
for your computer to catch up.

"Let your eyes leisurely look
at the flowers blooming and
falling in your courtyard.
Whether you leave or retain your
position, take no care. Let your
mind wander with the clouds
folding and unfolding beyond
the horizon."

—Hung Tzu-ch'eng
(1593–1665)

At the end of each day, drop
your change in a jar. Each
month, turn it in and use the
money to treat yourself to a
movie and a snack . . . alone.

Walk for twenty minutes
after dinner every night.

Glorious silence: Spend a
few minutes every day
without conversation,
music, or the news.

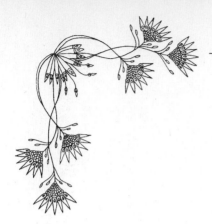

Wander downtown and get
your palm read. It's all in
fun and gives a little boost
to your daydreams.

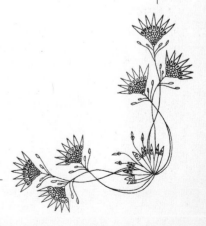

Always have a jar of jellybeans
or gumdrops nearby.

Take the night off and order
in from your favorite eatery.
Enjoy your meal in the
comfort of your own home.

Put down roots. Take your shoes off and walk on the grass, step in a puddle, or dangle your feet in a creek.

"*Moderation is a fatal thing.
Nothing succeeds like excess.*"

——*Oscar Wilde
(1854–1900)*

Buy yourself a new pair of
sneakers. This time, consider
blue, green, pink, or red instead
of standard-issue whites.
Then, watch your feet fly!

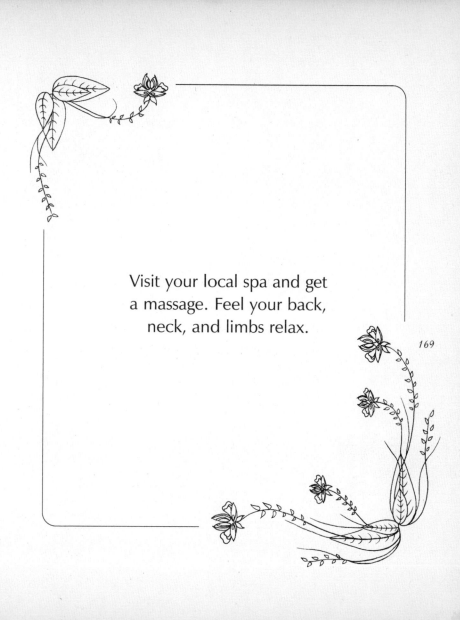

Visit your local spa and get
a massage. Feel your back,
neck, and limbs relax.

169

Place your bath towels on a warming rack and step out of the bath into toasty softness.

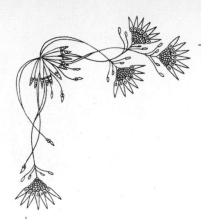

Find an Internet chat
room about one of your
passions (gardening, music,
movies, pets . . .).

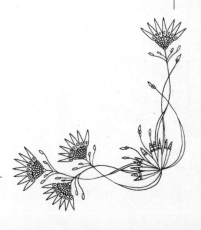

Break the routine by flipping
a coin next time you decide
to take a walk. Heads, you
turn right; tails, you turn left.
Repeat at each street corner.
Enjoy not knowing exactly
where you'll end up!

Go see the fireworks
or watch a parade in
a nearby small town.

173

Dance at home. It will get your heart rate up and give you a chance to try out your moves in front of a mirror. When ready, stop by your local dance club.

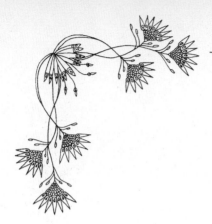

Use a desk or floor lamp at the office to offset the glare of fluorescence. Better yet, turn off the overhead lights altogether.

175

Freeze slices of your favorite
fruit in a Ziploc® bag for
a special treat every
time you have a drink.

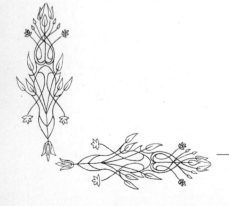

"The man is richest whose
pleasures are the cheapest."

—Henry David Thoreau
(1817–1862)

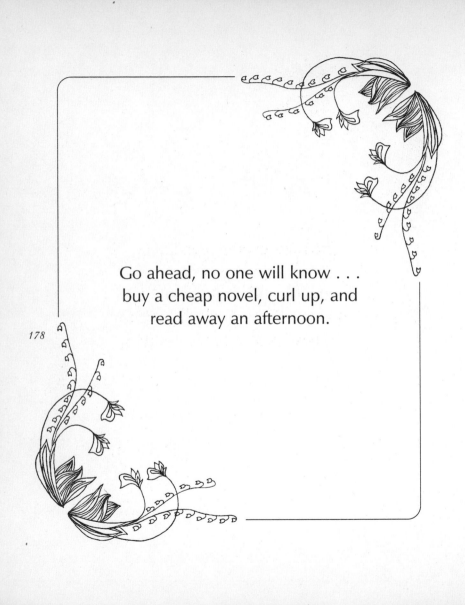

Go ahead, no one will know . . .
buy a cheap novel, curl up, and
read away an afternoon.

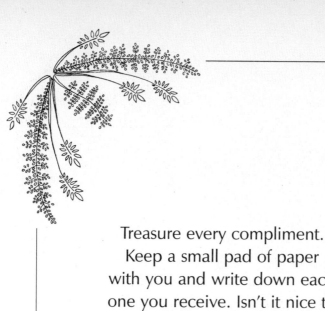

Treasure every compliment.
Keep a small pad of paper
with you and write down each
one you receive. Isn't it nice to
know you're appreciated?

Skip.

Yes, you need another pair of
shoes. Stop at your favorite store
and slip into something fabulous.

Hire a neighborhood teen to do your grocery shopping. Just jot down your list and hand it over. Let the younger generation do the searching and lugging.

181

Soft on the eyes. Hunt down
every 100-watt light bulb in your
house and replace it with a
gentle 60-watt bulb.

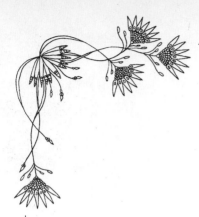

For a fun weekend getaway, drop your everyday car off for a tune-up and rent a more exciting car for the trip.

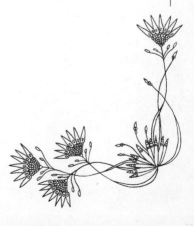

Skip stones on the water.

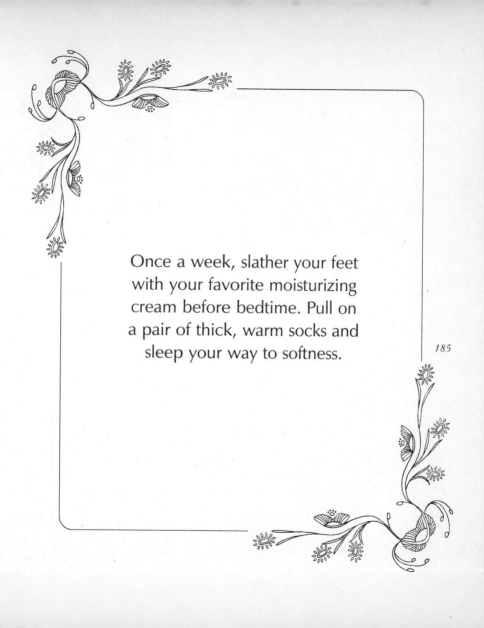

Once a week, slather your feet with your favorite moisturizing cream before bedtime. Pull on a pair of thick, warm socks and sleep your way to softness.

"Make everything as simple
as possible, but not simpler."

—Albert Einstein
(1879–1955)

Use a loofa mitt or
scrub puff every day for
bright, healthy skin.

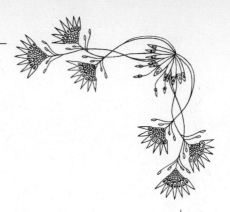

Keep a pair of comfy shoes
in your car. Slip off your high
heels every time you get
into the driver's seat.

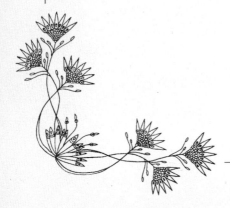

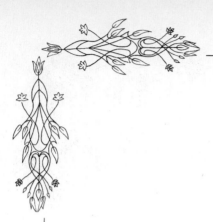

Plan next week's outfits from
your wardrobe. It saves time
and stress in the morning.

189

Keep a small pad with you
to write down your lists.
Why try to remember
everything you have to do?

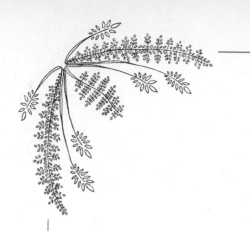

Cannonball into the pool.

Pamper your peeps. After an hour staring at the computer screen, take a visual yoga break. Focus on a spot across the room and open your eyes really wide. Then relax your face and let your jaw hang as you take deep breaths. It only takes a few seconds to feel ready to get back to work.

Every once in a while, get up early enough to greet the sunrise.

Record a loved one's voice telling your favorite stories from childhood. Hit the play button and let them tell you a "bedtime story" whenever you need a little mothering.

193

*"I try to avoid looking forward
or backward, and try to keep
looking upward."*

——*Charlotte Brontë
(1816—1855)*

Meditate. Each morning,
sit in a chair for ten minutes
with your feet flat on the ground
and your hands in your lap.
Pick a phrase or word that
soothes you. Repeat it under
your breath as you breathe in
and out. This is a great way to
start and end your day.

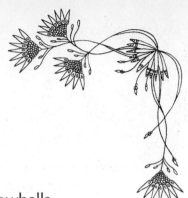

Throw snowballs.

Make snow angels.

Place colored stones in a
pretty clear bowl. Run your
fingers through the stones
when you feel tense.

Swing! Drop by your local
playground and see if you
can get going without a push.
How high can you go?

Four words:
bright red toenail polish.

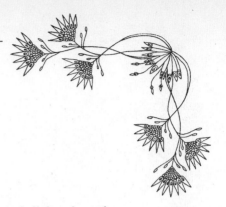

Treat yourself to a full-body salt scrub at your local spa. It exfoliates like nothing else and leaves your skin tingling for days. The silky softness lasts and lasts.

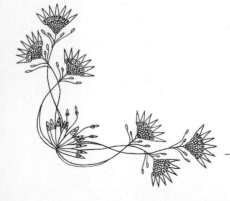

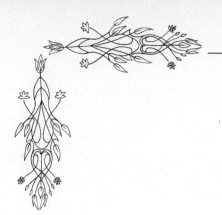

Sleep outside on a warm night.
Don't forget the air mattress!

201

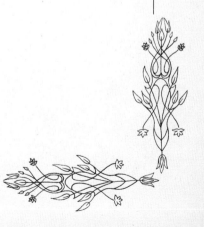

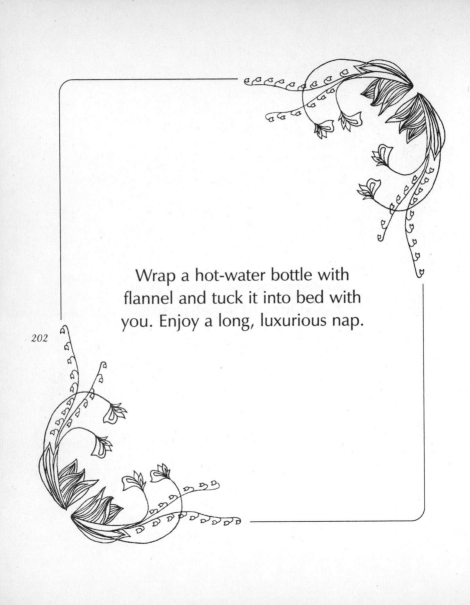

Wrap a hot-water bottle with
flannel and tuck it into bed with
you. Enjoy a long, luxurious nap.

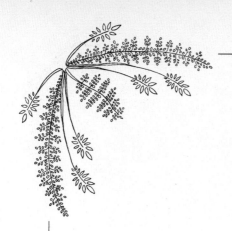

How about an entire
dinner of appetizers?

How about an entire
dinner of desserts?

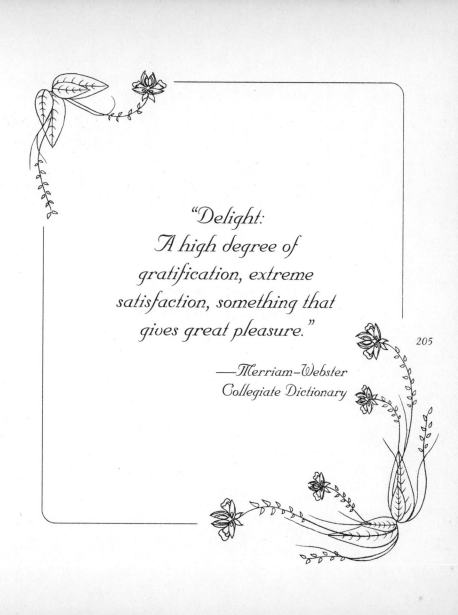

"Delight:
A high degree of
gratification, extreme
satisfaction, something that
gives great pleasure."

205

—*Merriam-Webster*
Collegiate Dictionary

Go to a used bookstore
and look for an old favorite.

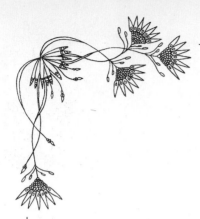

Get a babysitter on a day when
you don't have to be anywhere.

207

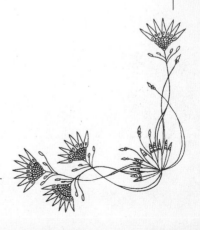

Get your eyebrows
professionally shaped. You'll
love the clean, groomed look.

Make your bed every
morning. You'll be
glad every night.

209

Snuggle time. Place a long body
pillow next to you at night for
extra support and comfort.

"*It is funny about life: if you refuse to accept anything but the very best you will very often get it.*"

——*W. Somerset Maugham*
(1874–1965)

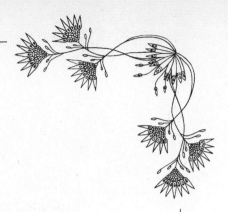

Toss out those old,
tired sunglasses and
shop for a new pair.

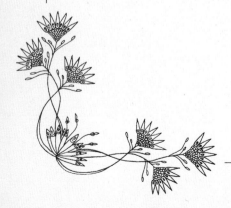

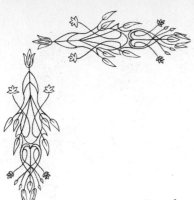

Cut fresh watermelon,
pineapple, or honeydew
into chunks and drop into
a pitcher of water. Chill for
two hours and serve this
delicious drink over ice.

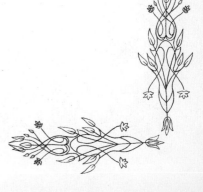

Examine your mirror image for
something other than flaws . . .
look for YOU.

Straighten up! Set your
shoulders back and down
directly over your hips. Lift
your chin. Feel that instant
energy and confidence!

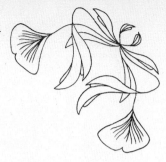

Trade in the imitation
syrup hiding in your cabinet
for *real* maple syrup.

Go fly a kite.

Did your mother have a favorite hand cream? Did your grandmother use a particular soap? Occasionally substitute for your favorites, and enjoy a blast from the past.

217

Delicious dip: one tub of cottage cheese, four tablespoons of dried minced onion, and a half teaspoon of garlic salt. Keep in the fridge to enjoy with celery or your favorite vegetable.

Take time to daydream.

Consider giving away all your
clothes that are "dry-clean only."

Power relax! Tense up all your muscles (remember to breathe!) for a few seconds and then let them go limp. It's really hard to be stressed out with all your muscles relaxed.

Carry a smaller purse. Enjoy the
freedom from the five-pound
sack you carry now.

You are not too old to have a "blankie." Find a soft, warm blanket to curl up in or under.

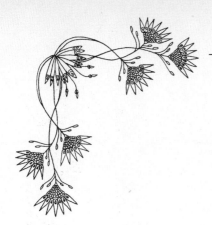

Stop by a store with great scents,
such as a tobacco, chocolate,
or candle shop. Go inside
and breathe deeply.

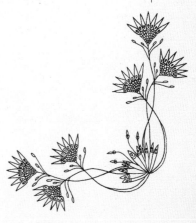

"Think highly of yourself,
because the world takes you
at your own estimate."

—Unknown

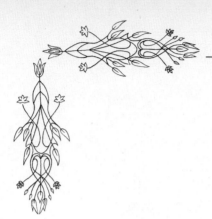

Give yourself a phone break.
Let the answering machine
take your calls until 8 P.M.
each evening.

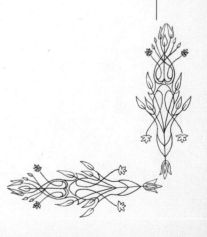

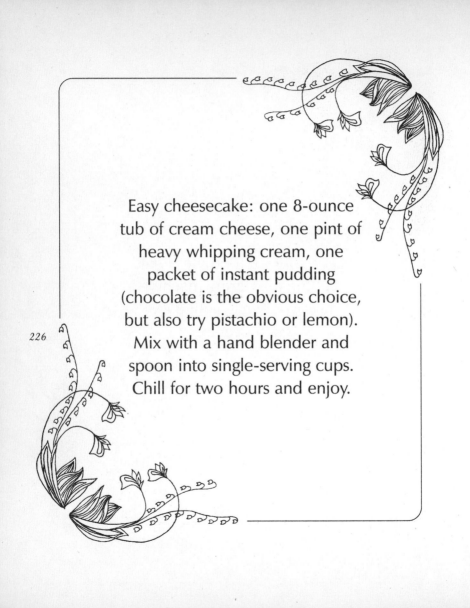

Easy cheesecake: one 8-ounce tub of cream cheese, one pint of heavy whipping cream, one packet of instant pudding (chocolate is the obvious choice, but also try pistachio or lemon). Mix with a hand blender and spoon into single-serving cups. Chill for two hours and enjoy.

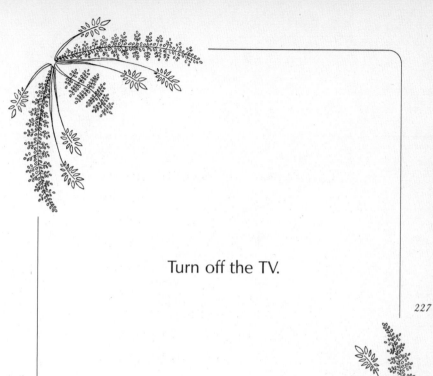

Turn off the TV.

Limber up for your day with
a long stretch after your
shower. The hot water
loosens up your muscles.

Rearrange your bedroom or
living room furniture. Voilà!—
a whole new home without
the hassle of moving.

229

Send yourself a letter listing
all your positive qualities.

Match your underwear colors
for a feminine boost.

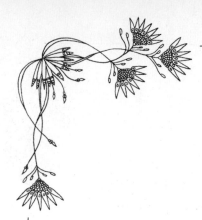

Peace of mind is easier in
peaceful surroundings. Pick just
one room and de-clutter!

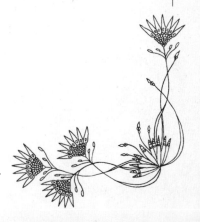

Use your good dishes.
If not now, when?

Make sure you take your
lunch break away from
the office or home.

If the worries and stresses
of the day are keeping you
awake, try this tip. Keep a
lavender-scented candle by your
bed and light it in the dark.
Focus on the flame as you
consciously "give" your worries
to it. When you are done, list off
the things you accomplished
today. Sweet dreams.

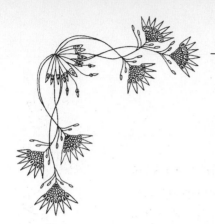

Tack your best fortune-cookie
fortune on the refrigerator.

"*Life isn't about finding yourself.*
Life is about creating yourself."

—George Bernard Shaw
(1856—1950)

Fill a shallow pan halfway with warm water and drop in several handfuls of smooth stones. Add a healthy splash of witch hazel and your favorite shower gel. Soak your feet for ten minutes while gently rubbing your soles over the stones.

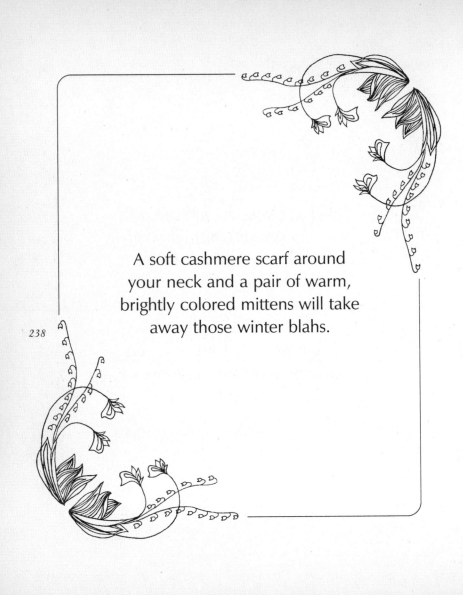

A soft cashmere scarf around
your neck and a pair of warm,
brightly colored mittens will take
away those winter blahs.

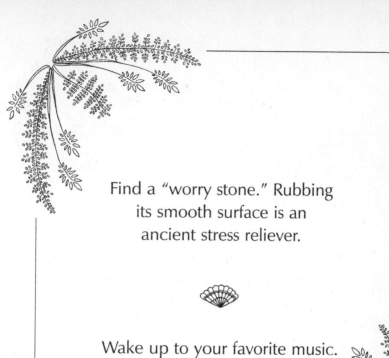

Find a "worry stone." Rubbing
its smooth surface is an
ancient stress reliever.

Wake up to your favorite music.

Call your local massage school
and sign up for a scalp massage.
You'll be set for the week.

Have a sleepover!

241

Celebrate spring by opening
all your windows. Let the
breezes blow through and
chase winter away.

Moisten a hand towel with
warm water and rub the cloth
with a piece of fresh ginger.
Roll the towel and relax with
it behind your neck, knees, or
in the small of your back to
help loosen your muscles and
soothe your skin.

For a healthy glow, put your favorite herbal tea to boil in a shallow pan of water. When the pan is boiling, carefully hold your face and neck in the steam. The antioxidants and the steam will clean your skin and help you breathe more deeply.

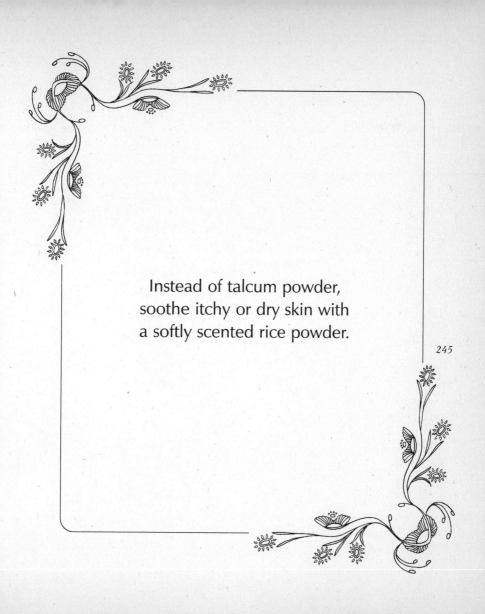

Instead of talcum powder,
soothe itchy or dry skin with
a softly scented rice powder.

Hang a Native American
dream catcher above
your bed for good luck.

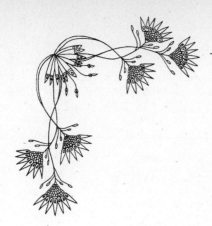

Have a long drive? Stop by your local library and check out their selection of books on tape. Those miles will just fly by.

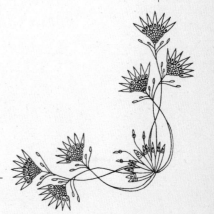

Before you go to bed each night,
step outside and look at the stars.

Spring is garage-sale time!
Tour your neighborhood
and look for fun bargains.

"Always look at what you have left.
Never look at what you have lost."

—*Rev. Robert H. Schuller*

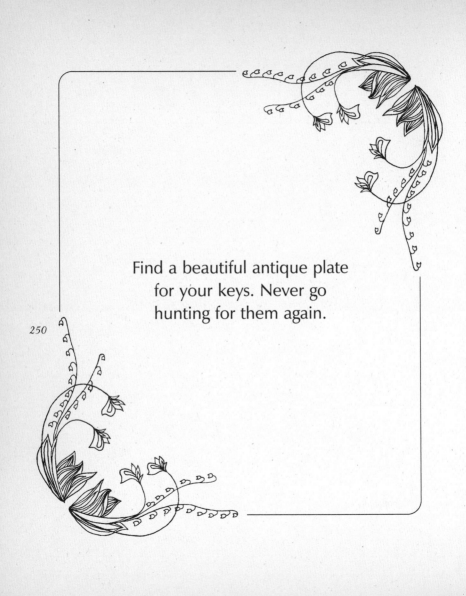

Find a beautiful antique plate
for your keys. Never go
hunting for them again.

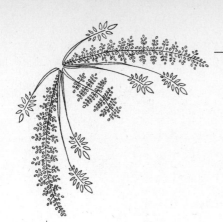

The best of bread! Thaw frozen
bread dough and let rise in the
refrigerator. Kneading bread
feels and smells great.

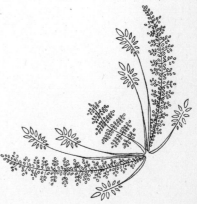

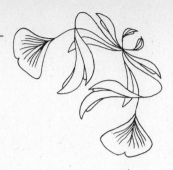

Breathe deeply. Close
the bathroom door, set
your shower to "hot," and let
the steam rise. Twenty minutes
in the warm steam will open
your pores and relax away
the stresses of the day.

Tell someone you love them.

Fresh-squeezed orange juice . . .
there is no substitute.

Pamper your clothes. Replace your old hangers with thick, silky padded ones. Your favorite outfits and sweaters will hang more beautifully and keep their shape better.

"Be happy.
It is a way of being wise."

——Colette

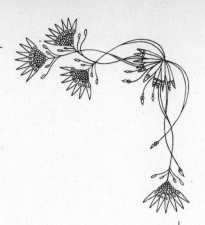

Take off your watch
at every opportunity.

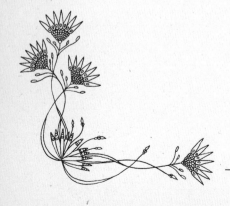

Add a dollop of pistachio
or pecan-mint ice cream
to your coffee for a
sweet, delicious treat.

257

Buy a mini sandbox
for your desk.

Small, white fairy lights
aren't just for the holidays.
String up a multitude of lights
across your porch ceiling or
railings for year-round cheer.

259

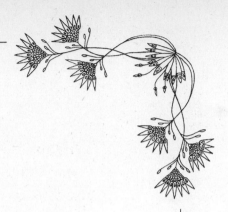

Throw out your scale.

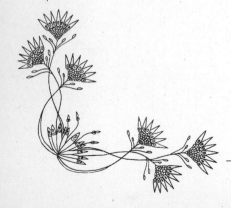

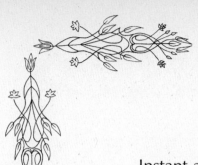

Instant artist! Pick up a watercolor kit. They are available everywhere and just the thing to get your artistic juices going. Spread newspapers on your kitchen table and play with colors. Painting is a soul-stretching activity that everyone can benefit from.

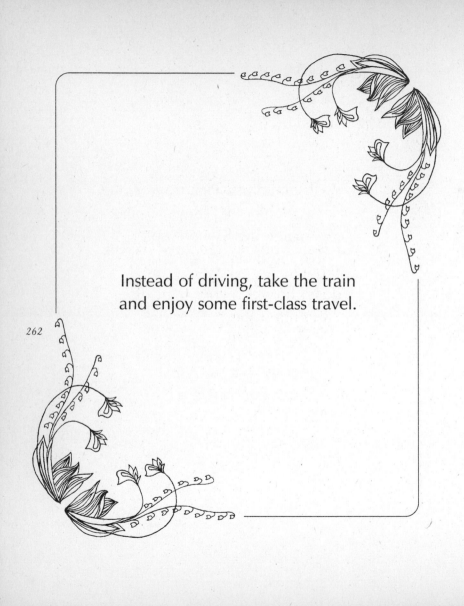

Instead of driving, take the train
and enjoy some first-class travel.

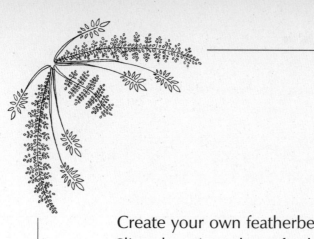

Create your own featherbed.
Slip a luxurious down-feather
duvet between your mattress
and fitted sheet. Surround
yourself with softness.

263

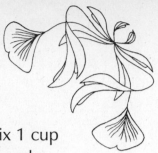

More blender beauty. Mix 1 cup melon and 1 cup pineapple with 3 cups of seltzer water in a blender. In the shower, pour the mixture into a wash-cloth and smooth it all over your body. Enzymes and vitamins will soak into your skin for two to three minutes. Rinse off and your skin will look and feel amazingly smooth.

"*Optimism is the one quality
more associated with success
and happiness than any other.*"

—Brian Tracy

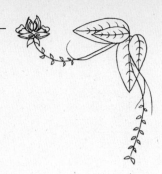

Get rid of call waiting.
It adds nothing to your life.

Experience the weather, don't hide from it. Leave the umbrella in the house. Feel the rain. Play in the snow. Bathe in the sun.

267

For a fragrant bath that restores,
mix 1 cup powdered milk with
a teaspoon each of orange peel,
dried rosemary, and dried or
fresh rose petals.

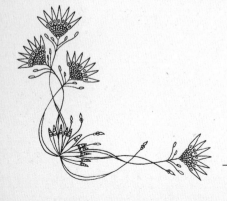

Spend an afternoon lounging in a hammock. Lay down a cotton blanket, add a few pillows, and sway until dusk.

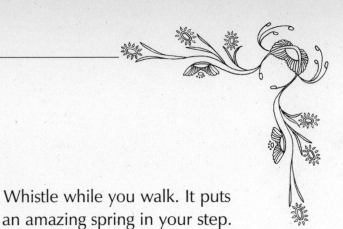

Whistle while you walk. It puts
an amazing spring in your step.

Sit in the garden and listen . . .
just listen.

List the things you are
grateful for in your life.

"I am beginning to learn that it is the sweet, simple things of life which are the real ones after all."

—Laura Ingalls Wilder
(1867—1957)